BIZLEY, K.

Surfing

Radical Sports
Surfing

Kirk Bizley •••••••••••

Heinemann
LIBRARY

www.heinemann.co.uk

Visit our website to find out more information about **Heinemann Library** books.

To order:
☎ Phone 44 (0) 1865 888066
▤ Send a fax to 44 (0) 1865 314091
▭ Visit the Heinemann Bookshop at www.heinemann.co.uk to browse our catalogue and order online.

First published in Great Britain by Heinemann Library,
Halley Court, Jordan Hill, Oxford OX2 8EJ,
a division of Reed Educational and Professional
Publishing Ltd.

Heinemann is a registered trademark of Reed Educational
& Professional Publishing Limited.

OXFORD   MELBOURNE   AUCKLAND
JOHANNESBURG   BLANTYRE   GABORONE
IBADAN   PORTSMOUTH NH (USA)   CHICAGO

Designed by Celia Floyd
Originated by HBM Print ltd, Singapore
Printed in Hong Kong by Wing King Tong

ISBN 0 431 03677 2 (hardback)
04 03 02 01 00
10 9 8 7 6 5 4 3 2 1

ISBN 0 431 03686 1 (paperback)
04 03 02 01 00
10 9 8 7 6 5 4 3 2 1

British Library Cataloguing in Publication Data

Bizley, Kirk
    Surfing. – (Radical sports)
    1. Surfing – Juvenile literature
    I. Title
    797.3'2

Acknowledgements

The Publishers would like to thank the following for
permission to reproduce photographs:

Allsport, p. 27 top (Todd Warshaw), p. 29 top (Jamie
Squire); Chris Power, pp. 23, 27 top, 28; Environmental
Images, p. 25 top; Ester Spears, p. 26; Estpix, p. 29
bottom; Hulton Getty, pp. 4, 5; Robert Ashton, pp. 6-21,
25 bottom.

Cover photograph reproduced with permission of Tony
Harrington/Stock Shot

Our thanks to Colin Wilson of the British Surfing
Association for his comments in the preparation of this
book.

Every effort has been made to contact copyright holders
of any material reproduced in this book. Any omissions
will be rectified in subsequent printings if notice is given
to the Publisher.

Any words appearing in the text in bold, **like this**, are
explained in the Glossary.

This book aims to cover all the essential techniques of
this radical sport but it is important when learning a new
sport to get expert tuition and to follow any
manufacturers' instructions.

797. 3

CONTENTS

INTRODUCTION

A short history

The islands of Hawaii were discovered by Captain James Cook in 1778. When he arrived there one of the islanders paddled out to greet him on a surfboard. This is the earliest recorded use of a surfboard. The surfboard used was a large slab of hardwood, much bigger and heavier than the boards we use today.

Where it all began

The sport of surfboarding began in the United States and Hawaii and there is a record of an Olympic gold medal swimmer called Duke Paoa Kahanamoku surfing at Santa Cruz in Northern California in 1885. But the official start of surfing was in 1907 at Redondo Beach in Southern California where it was introduced by George Freeth. In the same year in Hawaii the Outrigger Canoe Club was formed and surfing was one of the activities they offered.

Duke Paoa Kahanamoku at the Surf Board Swimming Championships in Honolulu in 1924. He is in the foreground with the surfboard marked 'Duke'.

Better boards

As the design of the surfboards changed, they became lighter and easier to carry and manoeuvre. As a result, the sport became more popular. By the 1930s the boards were made of plywood and balsa, and **fins** were added to help with steering. An American, Tom Blake, designed and rode the first light, hollowed out surfboard in 1928 off the Californian coast.

Surfers in Hawaii in the 1930s.

Later developments

The materials being used to make boards continued to become lighter, and the sport more popular. Also, the surfers were beginning to perform more and more manoeuvres on them. By the 1960s the boards were made of Styrofoam and **fibreglass**. Surfing took off particularly well in Australia and the United States, especially at Malibu in California.

In England the sport was introduced by Australian lifeguards (lifesavers) who had come over to work on the beaches in Cornwall. By 1966 the British Surfing Association had been formed.

The first World Amateur Championships were held in 1964 and the sport turned professional in 1970 when the first World Professional Championships were held.

BOARDS AND BASIC EQUIPMENT

You will obviously need a surfboard if you want to surf but if you're a beginner you might get very confused about what type to get. Surfboards are available in three basic types:

Soft boards

These are made of semi-rigid plastic foam that is very soft and very **buoyant**. Unlike other boards they don't have a hard glass finish but are extremely hard wearing.

Pop-out boards or moulded surfboards

These boards are made in a mould. They are made by joining two halves of moulded **fibreglass** together which is then filled in the middle with liquid **polyurethane** foam which sets and hardens. These are quite heavy but very hard wearing.

Custom surfboards

These are hand-made from polyurethane blanks which are shaped and then covered with a thin layer of fibreglass. They can be made to any shape, design or colour and are very light. However, they can be easily damaged, and they are the most expensive type!

The bodyboard

An alternative to all of the above is a bodyboard. This is a rectangular board made of polyethylene, designed just for the **prone** position or **drop knee** position.

Once you have your board there are a few of other pieces of equipment you should get.

Surfboard leash

This is a piece of stretchy cord that fixes on to the tail of your board at one end and onto your rear leg at the ankle at the other. It can also be called a leg rope. Make sure that it is the right length so that your board can't get too far away, or stay dangerously close.

Rail saver

Your leash should also have a **rail saver**. This is a flat nylon strip which fits between the board and the leash to prevent the leash from tearing through your surfboard and damaging the **rail**.

A leash should have an ankle strap and a rail saver.

Wax and deck grip

This is an essential extra if you have a hard board. You put **wax** on your board in order to help your feet grip it when you are surfing. A **deck grip** is also a good idea. Although it's more expensive than wax you only have to put it on once.

Nose guards

You can give your board some protection from scratches and **dings** by attaching rubber **nose guards** to it.

Boardbag

It would also be a good idea to buy a **boardbag**. This is a padded bag that you can store and carry your board in.

Wax is made from a combination of paraffin and beeswax and you can get different degrees of hardness for different water temperatures.

THE BOARD FOR YOU

Once you have decided which type of board you want to buy you then have to decide on some other details, such as how much you want to spend.

Second-hand boards

As boards are quite expensive it might be a good idea to buy a good second-hand one, which you can usually get for about half the price of a new one.

If you do decide to do this then try to take someone along who knows about surfboards to help you, but there are also some signs you can check for.

- Look for any soft spots where the **fibreglass** is coming away from the foam.
- Make sure there are no cracks around the bottom of the board, especially where the **fins** are joined on.
- Don't buy a board that is going yellow or discoloured. This means that water has got into the foam core of the board and is 'waterlogged'. A board in this condition will not last very long!

Correct length

If you're a beginner you don't need a top-of-the-range, expensive board – it probably would not be the best for you. You will need a board that floats you adequately and is stable in the water. It should be about 300–450 mm longer than you are.

Choosing the right length of board is important when selecting a board.

Learning how to surf at a surf school with other beginners is the best way to start the sport.

Where to go

The most common boards for beginners are **soft boards** and these are used by most of the **surf schools**. If you're thinking of taking up the sport, it would be a good idea to go along to a surf school where you will be able to try out the different types of board and get some basic instruction and guidance as well.

Prices of boards vary a lot and from area to area, so it's a good idea to shop around for the best buy.

There is a large range of surfboards to choose from so it's best to get some expert advice at a specialist surf shop or surf school.

WHAT ELSE DO YOU NEED?

As with other surfing purchases you will have a choice of clothing types and styles. What you need will depend upon when and where you want to surf.

Wetsuit

For a beginner, a double-lined suit is ideal and you can get a different thickness for different times of the year. For the summer, 2 to 3 millimetres will be enough and you will probably not need legs or arms on the suit. For the winter, the thickness should be 4 to 5 millimetres and it's best to have full-length arms and legs on the suit rather than 'cut-offs'.

summer wetsuit

winter wetsuit

Rash vest

You should wear a **rash vest** under your wetsuit. This prevents the rubber chaffing on your shoulders and underarms when **paddling**. Rash vests are made of close-fitting lycra and can be useful protection from the sun if worn on their own in hot climates.

Extra protection

Apart from a wetsuit you can get additional protective clothing made from **neoprene** rubber, including boots, gloves and hoods.

Boots

Boots can help to protect your feet, especially from the sharp rocks at reefs and the spikes of sea urchins. Again, you must make sure that they are a very good fit otherwise they will fill up like balloons on your feet!

Gloves

You can get gloves that are like fingerless mittens and these can make paddling more comfortable.

Hood

A hood can protect your head and ears from the cold or from any knocks off the board. It's also possible to buy specific surf helmets. These are made from **fibreglass** so are lightweight. They offer the best head protection.

Most people surfing in cooler places such as Britain in the winter months would need all of this protective clothing.

SAFETY FIRST

A wetsuit protects you from cuts and abrasions caused from catching the board or hitting the water.

PRE-SURF CHECKS AND PREPARATION

Surfing is not a simple matter of getting onto a board and getting on with it. You have to build up to that. Before you surf you should always carefully check all of your equipment and the conditions of the water. One of the best ways to check the conditions is to spend about ten minutes just watching the surf and the other surfers.

SAFETY FIRST

Before you surf, make sure you can swim! You will be **paddling** out to sea, out of your depth and you can't just rely on being able to use your board as a float, you need to be a competent swimmer!

Safe places

If you're a beginner you should only surf at beaches that are under the supervision of qualified lifeguards (lifesavers) and always stay within the appropriate flags. Keep an eye on where these flags are – ask one of the lifeguards if you're in any doubt.

Watching the surf and other surfers is always a good idea before you start to surf yourself. Look out for waves breaking on rocks or other hazards and **rip currents**.

Equipment check

At this point you should make sure that your wetsuit is on properly. If you have a hard board without a **deck grip**, check that you have **waxed** all over the top of the board.

Warm-up

The final thing you must do is a **warm-up** and you should spend about 10 minutes doing this. If you have cold, stiff muscles you could have problems with cramp when you are out in the water, so spend some time preparing them. You should also cool-down for 10 minutes after your surf to stop you aching the next day.

Calf and back stretch

Stretch down to reach your toes with one hand. Hold this stretch for 5 seconds then straighten up and stretch to the other foot. Repeat this 10 times.

Hamstring stretch

Standing on one leg pull the other up behind you. Hold this position for 10 seconds then do the other leg.

◄········ *Inner thigh stretch*

Sit down placing the soles of your feet together. Gently lean forwards. Hold this position for 10 seconds then relax.

BASIC TECHNIQUES

Only when you have finished all of your pre-surf checks and preparation should you even think about getting into the water.

Carrying the board

Make sure that you carry your board down to the water carefully and safely. The best way to do this is to carry it with the **fins** forward and facing towards your body, and the **leash** (leg rope) neatly tied around it.

When you get down to the edge, untie the leash from around your board and put it on securely. It should go on under your wetsuit, with the cord facing outwards.

Don't push the board in front of you as a wave could knock it into you, and don't lift it over the waves – just let it float over them.

Into the sea

Now you're ready to carry your board out through the broken waves. Just let the board float beside you, with the front pointing out to sea.

Keep both of your hands on the board. You want to partly balance on the board as you walk out, especially if you're walking over some rough rocks.

SAFETY FIRST

Never surf alone. But don't get too close to other surfers, especially beginners!

Riding a wave lying down

Once you are waist deep you can get on your board
and try some basic surfing in the shallower **white water**.

Keep watching the waves
coming in from in front of you
until one is about 3 metres
away from you, then swing
your board around to face the
beach and lift yourself onto it
and lie centrally.

Simple, basic surfing in shallow water is a
good way to build up your basic surfing skills.

You must make sure that no one
else is riding in on the same
wave. As the wave gets closer
start to **paddle** with your hands
at the sides of the board. If you
get your timing right the wave will catch you and your
board, and lift the board up and push you forward in
towards the beach. Grip both sides of your board sliding
your weight down towards the back of it. If the **nose** of
the board goes up too high you may need to slide
forwards and remember to keep your head up to see
what's coming. To stop, all you have to do is slide off
your board.

You can practise
some basic steering
by moving your body
to the right and left.
See how it changes
the direction of the
board as it moves
towards the shore.

ARE YOU READY TO STAND?

1 Lie with your feet just over the end of the board, with your hands at the side.

Being able to stand up on your surfboard and surf-in is probably what you most want to do but you have to be prepared to take your time in learning how to do it.

Standing position

It's a good idea to practise getting up into the standing position with your board on the beach first, so that you know how to do it when you're on your board out at sea.

Place your board down on the sand (be careful with the **fins**) and go through this series of moves.

2 Put your hands on the board and raise the top of your body.

4 Place your front knee under your head, keeping both of your feet apart and well balanced. In the sea you may only be able to get to your knees at this point.

3 Slide your feet forward so that you are in a crouching position.

5 Get yourself into your standing surfing position, still with your body slightly crouched and your arms out to the side to keep balance.

Now for the sea!

You're now ready to practise in the water. You don't have to go too far out to. Indeed, it's a good idea to use the shallower, **white water** that you used for practising the basic skills of catching a wave and surfing in on your stomach. Repeat those basic steps, but at the point when your board is lifted by the wave you must try out the sequence of moves you practised on the beach – and attempt to get up on your feet. Don't worry if you only get up to your knees at first, even this is good balancing practice.

Don't expect to be able to do this first time. Be prepared to keep trying again until you can get yourself up into that standing, surfing position! You probably won't be able to surf for very far as you will be starting quite close to the beach, but five seconds or so is a very good beginning and will enable you to move on to the next stage.

SAFETY FIRST

- Check for any warning flags on the beach.

- Before going into the sea with your board always get advice about the conditions from lifeguards or other experts with local knowledge.

When you're in the water you can gradually build up from kneeling to standing.

OUT TO SEA!

Practise the basic techniques fairly close to the shore on broken waves, until you can steer, stand and stop. When you can do all this you're ready to go farther out to the **unbroken waves**.

Paddling out

Paddling out is the technique you need to get your board out. Push your board out as you normally would until you are about waist deep and then get on it, still facing out to sea. Lie on the board centrally so that the **nose** of the board is just clear of the water. Keep your legs together on the board and paddle using your arms just like a crawl swimming stroke. Keep your head up so that you can see where you are going.

Paddling out can take a long time and be very tiring.

Duck diving

As you go farther out you have to get past bigger and bigger **white water** and unbroken waves. To get past them you will have to learn **duck diving**. This involves sinking your board right under the oncoming waves and coming up the other side. If you can get the board deep enough under the wave it will prevent you getting dragged back towards the beach.

Duck diving will help you and your board to get past an oncoming wave.

The proper way to do this is to paddle hard towards the oncoming wave. Just before the wave hits you get hold of the **side rails** of the board under your chest, lift your backside and lean forwards, straightening your arms at the same time. This will start to sink the nose of the board and you should then bring one of your knees up under your body and push the board down and forwards under the water. Once the wave has passed over, you will begin to bob back up.

DROP IN

It's important that you never **drop in** on another surfer. This is when you take off on a wave somebody else is already riding.

You will know when you are far enough out because people will be **lining up**. They will be sitting on their boards and it's a good idea if you do the same.

Take off

This is a good time to watch the other surfers to see where they are **taking off** and how the waves are breaking. You have to get the wave just right to take off and it needs to be just as the wave is **peeling** or beginning to form.

To take off follow the same technique you used in the shallower water and see if you can get onto your feet and stay up as long as possible as you surf in.

You need to take the opportunity when the right wave comes along.

CARING FOR YOUR EQUIPMENT

It's unlikely that any of your surf equipment was cheap so it's important that you look after it very carefully.

Safe places

You should never leave your board lying around in strong sunlight or locked inside a car at the height of summer. Extreme heat or direct sunlight will discolour the foam and it can cause the foam or **fibreglass** to deteriorate. The shiny laminate covering might also break up. If you have a padded **boardbag** make sure you use it.

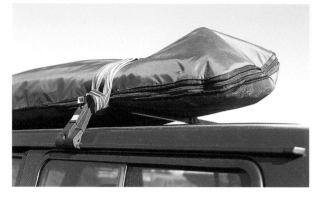

When transporting your board (usually on a car roof, or luggage rack) make sure that any securing straps don't put too much pressure on the board.

Repairing your board

You can be sure that your board will collect **dings**. These dents or holes are easily made if you drop your board or knock it into something when surfing. Dings should be repaired otherwise they will allow the water to seep into your board and cause more damage.

You may be able to repair these yourself using a fibreglass repair kit. You can make an emergency temporary repair by putting some duct tape over the hole or by filling the hole with **wax** to seal it.

If the damage is more than you can cope with or you're not sure you can repair it, take it to a surf shop and let them do the job for you!

Waxing

Never wax your board on a hard surface. This can mark the bottom of the board and very easily damage the **fins**.

Wetsuit maintenance

Your wetsuit also needs careful maintenance if it's to last. Always be careful when putting on and taking off your wetsuit so as not to over stretch or tear the **neoprene**.

After surfing, always rinse your wetsuit in fresh water and let it dry. You can even wash it in a washing machine on a very gentle wash. Don't leave it lying around in strong sunlight and always roll it up if you have to pack it.

Put on your wetsuit gradually, rolling and sliding it on. Be equally careful when taking it off.

Be very careful when you pull the zips up. Don't pull hard on them if they appear to be stuck.

SAFETY

Surfing is an exciting and exhilarating sport – but it can also be very dangerous. Because of the dangers there are a lot of safety rules that you must know and you must follow!

Any surfing association will tell you that you should have an extensive knowledge of the sea and water safety. You should attend a first aid or life saving course.

This is the advice given to all surfers:
- Never surf alone.
- Always tell someone where your are going to surf and approximately what time you expect to return.
- Never surf immediately after taking food or alcohol.
- Never attempt a rescue if it will put you in danger.
- Always watch out for other surfers – especially beginners.
- Don't stay in the water when you start to feel cold.
- Always know the location of **rip currents**.

Rip currents

Rip currents are areas where a gully fills with water and then rushes out to sea. These gullies, or channels, are usually found near rocks, rivers, sand banks and piers. One of the problems with them is that they can occur without warning and without there being an obvious source. However, remember that the bigger the surf the stronger the current will be.

Some signs and indications of a rip current are:
- discoloured water due to sand movement
- waves break out at sea and then back off again, becoming an unbroken wave
- debris and rubbish floating out to sea
- a rippled appearance on the surface of the sea
- foam on the surface, moving out to sea.

If you do get caught in a rip current:
- don't panic and don't let go of your board
- don't try to **paddle** against the rip current, just paddle at 90 degrees to it and then paddle back to the shore
- if the rip current is too strong, paddle out to sea and signal for help by raising one arm above your head and then wait for the emergency services
- there may be no immediate sign of a rip current so always be prepared.

Getting advice

When you go to any beach the best thing is to get some local advice from some of the other swimmers or from the lifeguards (lifesavers) – they will all be happy to help. You should also look out for the flags on the beach that give you information. But flags can differ from country to country so you should check locally before starting to surf.

Check with the local lifeguard about sea conditions before starting to surf.

SURFING RULES AND HAZARDS

When you are surfing you need to think about yourself and all of the other surfers because everyone wants to be having fun but they all want to be safe as well.

Because of this there are accepted codes of conduct which all surfers are asked to read, learn and stick to. This is the code of conduct issued by the British Surfing Association.

1 You must be able to swim at least 50 metres in open water.

2 Ensure that you are covered by Public Liability Insurance for surfing.

3 Keep your surfing equipment in good condition.

4 Always wear a surf **leash** (leg rope) to prevent you from losing your surfboard or bodyboard. Your board is a safety device for you but to others it may be a lethal weapon.

5 Have consideration for other water users, including anglers.

6 Never surf alone or after eating a meal.

7 Always return to the beach before nightfall.

8 Never mix surfing with alcohol or drugs.

9 Always wear a wetsuit when surfing in Britain.

10 If you are new to the sport, never hire a surfboard without first having a surfing lesson (given by a qualified instructor).

11 Be considerate of other beach users, especially when carrying your board to and from the water.

12 When possible use a lifeguard (lifesaver) patrolled beach. Obey the lifeguard's instructions and be prepared to help them if required.

13 Where possible surf in a recognized surfing area.

14 When **paddling out** avoid surfers who are riding waves.

15 When taking a wave see that you are clear of other surfers. Remember, if someone else is already riding the wave you must not **take off**.

16 Be environmentally friendly. Always leave the beach and other areas as you would wish to find them.

You would be well advised to join a surfing association if you intend to take up surfing. If you join the British Surfing Association you will get the public liability insurance you need free and this insurance is valid world-wide.

Pollution

This can be a real problem at some beaches – there can be sewage or industrial pollution in the sea water. You can contract unpleasant illnesses, such as an upset stomach, from surfing in this kind of seawater. Although there have been improvements, not all beaches are safe.

Polluted beaches and areas are not suitable places to surf – no matter how good the surf is!

Danger from the sun

Being out in the open, on a beach and in and out of the sea for long periods involves a real risk of over exposure to the sun. You must use a sunscreen cream and a waterproof sunblock for when you are in the water. Alternatively, you need to cover yourself up.

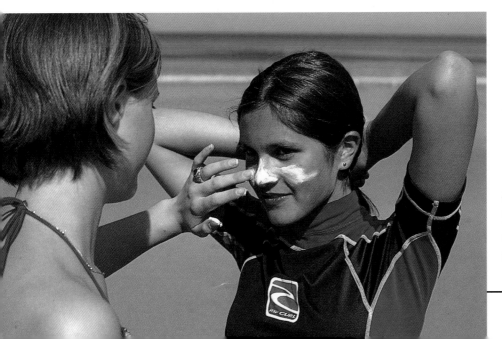

Protecting yourself from the sun is an absolute necessity when surfing.

TAKING IT FURTHER

If you would like to take up surfing, here is some information about how to go about it and about the types of competitions you could then get involved in.

Surf schools

The first thing you should do is to go to a **surf school**. Many schools exist. For example, there are 24 approved centres in Britain. You can contact the British Surfing Association to get their details.

If you go along to a surf school you will get good tuition and guidance from professional instructors who will save you a lot of time in the long run because they will be able to teach you all the basics.

Junior schemes

Once you have the basic skills you can look out for further training schemes. In the UK you can take part in the Young Athlete Junior Scheme. This helps you to learn to surf safely and quickly and covers five levels of various surfing skills, including beach safety, surfing theory and freestyle surfing manoeuvres. To take part in this scheme you need to be aged between seven and seventeen. You will be given a log book and certificates of achievement as you progress through the levels.

Competitions in Britain

Surfing is a popular and successful sport in Britain and there have been organized competitions since 1966.

A British surfer, Rodney Sumpter won the World Junior Championship in 1967. Since then there have been a great many British successes. By the 1980s there were events such as the 'Fosters and Hot Tuna Surfmasters', held at Fistral Beach, Newquay, which attracted the top surfers in the world. One of them was a British born surfer, Martin Potter, who went on to win the world title in 1989.

Competitive surfing is the best way to try your skills out against other surfers.

Lee Bartlett, a BSA champion, in action.

THE INTERNATIONAL SCENE

Surfing has grown as a sport very rapidly since it first became popular in the 1960s. It's now an international sport with professional surfers from all over the world. In Australia, for example, surfing competitions for all ages are held all year round. One of the most famous is held at Bell's Beach, Victoria in Australia every April.

World Championship Tour

For senior surfers there are a dozen events in eight countries for the World Qualifying Series. These determine which of the sixteen surfers move up a level to the World Championship Tour.

The Association of Surfing Professionals (ASP) organizes the sport internationally and events are held all over the world. One of these is known as the 'Pipe Masters' which is the final event of the ten-month long World Championship Tour. This event has been running for 27 years.

One of the most successful surfers in the world is Kelly Slater. He has won the men's World Tour six times!

Junior World Championships

The ASP has recently started a Junior Tour which is split into regions throughout the world. In 1998 the six top surfers from all of the regions attended the Junior World Championships in Hawaii.

The Triple Crown

The Triple Crown is the second most important event to the ASP world title and it's one of the most coveted titles in surfing. This is because it's won by the surfer who is the best and most consistent in Hawaiian conditions. Here the seas can be huge open ocean swells, alongside coral and lava reefs. Some of

A surfer taking the challenge of the Hawaiian waves in the Swatch Aloha Wave Classic Competition in 1998.

the waves can break as far as half a mile out to sea. Such seas are thought by many to be the ultimate challenge!

World Surfing Games

The World Surfing Games are held every two years and features teams of surfers from all over the world. Over 40 countries took part in the event when it was held in California in 1996.

Australian Dean Morrison at the World Surfing Games in 1998.

GLOSSARY

boardbag   a padded bag used for carrying and storing your board in

buoyant   floats well

custom surfboard   the most expensive type of board which is hand-made to suit an individual's needs

deck grip   a rubber patch that sticks on your board to give you extra grip

dings   dents or holes in a surfboard

drop in   when one surfer takes off on a wave that is already being ridden by another surfer

drop knee   balancing on one knee on your body board

duck diving   a method of getting through a breaking or broken wave while you are paddling out

fibreglass   a material made from fine glass fibres

fin   a projection at the bottom of the board that helps with steering

leash   also called a leg rope. A cord that is attached to the board and the surfer's ankle by a strap

lining up   surfers sitting on their boards out at sea, waiting to catch a wave

moulded boards   also known as pop-out boards, these are boards that are made by joining two halves of moulded fibreglass and filling them with foam

neoprene   elastic material that acts as an insulator even when wet

nose   the front end of the board

nose guards   rubber guards fitted to the end, or nose, of the board

paddling   the method used to get your board out to sea

paddling out   lying on the board and paddling it out to sea

peeling   a wave that breaks evenly and cleanly from its peak

polyurethane   a tough protective coating applied to surfboards

pop-out boards   another name for moulded boards

prone   lying down flat on the board

rails   the sides of the board

rail saver   leash attachment which stops the leash cutting through the sides of the board

rash vest   a protective vest made of lycra and worn underneath a wetsuit

rip currents   a channel of water that runs out to sea

side rails   the two sides of a surfboard

soft board   semi-rigid plastic foam board. It is the basic type of board and ideal for beginners

surf school   a specially organized training school for surfers

taking off   the beginning of a ride when a wave is caught

unbroken waves   an area out at sea where waves have not yet fully formed

warm-up   a series of exercises and movements to prepare your body for surfing

wax   a combination of paraffin and beeswax that is put on a surfboard to help with grip

white water   water near the shore where the wave has begun to break

wipe out   being knocked off, or falling off your board by the force of a wave

USEFUL ADDRESSES

British Surfing Association
Champions Yard
Penzance
Cornwall
TR18 2TA
Telephone: 01736 360 250
Fax: 01736 331 077
E-mail colin@britsurf.demon.co.uk
(further details about all of the surf clubs
and groups can be obtained from the
BSA)

Scottish Surfing Federation
Chris Noble
20 Strichen Road,
Fraserburgh
AB43 5QZ

Welsh Surfing Federation
Linda Keward
29 Sterry Road
Gowerton
Swansea
SA4 3BS

Irish Surfing Association
Roci Allen
1 Ardealan Dale
Rossnowlagh
Co. Donegal
Ireland

Federation Francaise de Surf
BP 28 Plage Nord 40150
Hossegor
France

Surfing Australia
National Office
PO Box 1055
Burleigh Heads
Queensland 4220
Australia

FURTHER READING

Books

Surfing: The Fundamentals, Jeff Toghill, New Holland Publishers

Surfing Adventurers, Jeremy Evans, Prentice Hall & IBD

Websites

www.surfbus.freeserve.co.uk
(Magic Surf Bus)

www.surfstation.co.uk
(Surfstation)

www.surfingaustralia.com.au
(Surfing Australia)

www.britsurf.org
(UK surf index)

INDEX